dealing with
STRESS

Emma Haughton

Wayland

Bullying

Eating Disorders

Relationships

Substance Abuse

Death

Family Break-up

Stress

Peer Pressure

Thanks to Joff for all his help and support.

Editor: Alison Cooper

Series editor: Deborah Elliott

Concept design: Joyce Chester

Book design: Helen White

First published in 1995 by

Wayland (Publishers) Ltd

61 Western Road, Hove,

East Sussex BN3 1JD

British Library Cataloguing in Publication
Data

Haughton, Emma

  Dealing With Stress

  I. Title

  155.9042

ISBN 0 7502 1747 2

Typeset by White Design

Printed and bound by Canale in Italy

All of the people who appear in the
photographs in this book are models.
Commissioned photographs arranged
by Zoë Hargreaves.

Acknowledgements

Thanks to the staff and pupils of Blatchington Mill School, Hove, East Sussex, and to the following organizations which supplied the photographs used in this book: Cephas 11 (Stuart Boreham), 15 (Mick Rock), 24 (Mick Rock), 29 (Stuart Boreham), 44 (Stuart Boreham); Eye Ubiquitous 34 (J Burke), 38 (J Burke); Robert Harding 6-7, 22, 33, 35, 37; Rex Features 4 (Today), 5, 36 (Kim Ludbrook); Tony Stone Images 8 (Penny Tweedie), 19 (Gerard Loucel), 25 (Graeme Harris), 27 (Dale Durfee), 39 (David Young Wolff), 40 (Graeme Harris), 42 (Jean-Paul Nacivet), 43 (Don Smetzer), 45 (Andre Perlstein); Wayland Picture Library *cover* (APM Studios), 9 (APM Studios), 10 (APM Studios), 13 (APM Studios), 18 (Context), 21 (Context), 23, 26 (APM Studios), 28 (APM Studios), 30 (APM Studios), 31 (Tim Woodcock), 41 (Context); Zefa 16-17, 20, 32.

Contents

What is stress?

It's been said that the only people who aren't stressed, are dead! Stress is the tension you feel before you run on to the field for an important match, or the feeling of pressure as you try to find time to do your homework, go out with your friends *and* keep your parents happy by doing the washing-up.

It's a normal part of everyday life; it keeps you alert, helps you perform better and prepares you to face unfamiliar situations. Stress only becomes a problem when it gets out of control.

People can cope with varying amounts and types of stress. You might thrive under pressure, while a friend crumples under the strain. Too little happening in your life can be as stressful as too much. It's also a question of attitude: if you believe you can deal with a difficult situation, you won't get as stressed as someone who thinks they can't.

▲ **Stress helps people to perform better in challenging situations.**

There are some events in life, though, that most people find stressful: bereavement, divorce, illness, moving house, changing schools, exams, even holidays. Change disrupts the habits and routines that help people to cope with life without too much effort.

Stress and adolescents

Many teenagers feel stressed. You are entering an adult world that often seems to be full of confusion, violence and destruction. Just turning on the television or opening a news-paper can be an ordeal. Older people have the experience to understand that life goes on, however dreadful the news might be, but it's natural to feel pessimistic about the future at times.

Life is competitive, and involves a great deal of change. Young people have to form new relation-ships and fit into the world of work. At the same time, they have to deal with a rapidly changing body and many unfamiliar experiences and feelings.

Being different can be stressful – perhaps because you are disabled, or from a racial, ethnic or religious minority, or because you are gay or bisexual. Life is harder if you're homeless, in care, poor or unemployed. Bereavement, the divorce or break-up of your parents, and

physical, emotional or sexual abuse are all traumatic experiences. Having parents with problems such as disability, alcoholism or mental illness can also make you feel stressed.

▲ **Life is particularly stressful for young people living on the streets.**

Symptoms

Our minds might be fairly well adapted to modern life, but our bodies are comparatively prehistoric. When we feel threatened, our bodies release a hormone called adrenalin to help us fight off danger or flee from it. The heart races, breathing becomes faster and lighter, we sweat and our muscles tense up. This stress reaction is useful when facing sudden physical danger. If the threat or stress is a mental or emotional one, though, it puts great strain on our bodies; it's not usually appropriate in this kind of situation to release the tension by fighting or running away.

Everyday stress can cause other symptoms such as headaches or tiredness. Some people tense areas of their body, such as their fists or shoulders. Long-term stress can raise blood pressure and damage the body's immune system, and it is linked to problems such as heart disorders, stomach ulcers and cancer. Highly-stressed people are also more likely to have accidents.

Depression

Stress can affect your emotions, making you moody, irritable, or worried. You might have difficulty concentrating or sleeping properly. Long-term anxiety can lead to depression, estimated to affect up to 6 per cent of people aged fourteen to sixteen.

Depressed people might feel sad, worthless or powerless over many weeks or months. Some feel guilty, brooding over supposed faults or past mistakes. Others feel tired and listless, lose interest in hobbies and activities, sleep a lot or find it difficult to sleep at all. Some teenagers feel distanced from family and friends. Loss of interest and difficulty in concentrating can badly affect school work.

Depression in adolescence can show itself in other ways. Physical problems such as headaches or stomach aches can sometimes be a symptom of depression. For some teenagers, drug or alcohol abuse, promiscuity, crime, truanting or running away from home can all be ways of taking their mind off their problems. For many sufferers, these are also ways of calling attention to their inner distress.

Sometimes, depression is a reaction to a particularly stressful event; at other times it builds up with no obvious cause. Many people expect teenagers to be moody and emotional, and often a depressed teenager's behaviour is dismissed as 'just a phase'. People can be very unsympathetic, telling you to 'snap out of it' or 'pull yourself together'. But depression is more than 'normal' moodiness and it is serious. Immediate help, such as

counselling, psychotherapy or medication, will make recovery quicker and easier.

Suicide

Feelings of depression can become overwhelming, and you might want to 'find a way out'. You might believe no one cares about you, that your family and friends would be better off without you, or that life is pointless, hopeless or too painful to bear.

Tom, sixteen, was chucked by his girlfriend just before his GCSEs. When he failed in three subjects, he stopped seeing friends and sat in his room all day, drinking and smoking. One evening, Tom took all his mother's sleeping tablets from her bedroom drawer and washed them down with a four-pack of beer. He was lucky. He was sick and his mother found him soon afterwards.

Although most suicide attempts fail, suicide still accounts for 8 per cent of all deaths of people aged between fifteen and nineteen. Suicidal people need urgent help. About half of all children who kill themselves talk about or attempt suicide in the twenty-four hours before their death. They are not just attention-seeking or acting on impulse. Many teenage suicides are carefully planned.

▲ Many teenagers are moody and emotional but depression is much more serious than this. Sufferers can't just 'snap out of it' and they need urgent help.

If you have suicidal thoughts or feelings, go to your parents, doctor or teacher, or ring the Samaritans, an organization that runs a 24-hour helpline for those in distress. You will find the number in your phone book. Explain how you feel and ask for help. A counsellor or psychotherapist can help you through depression until life seems less bleak and you have more faith in yourself. Sometimes medication from your doctor can tide you over the worst until you are ready to tackle your problems. Never attempt suicide as a cry for help – you could do yourself a lot of damage.

You might know someone who seems very down, who perhaps says he or she would be better off dead or that no one would miss him or her. He or she might be obsessed with death, give away possessions, or take unnecessary risks. Urge a person in this state to get help. If he or she refuses, tell his or her parents or a teacher. You might prevent a lot of grief and pain.

Suicide is difficult to carry out and leaves family and friends with a terrible burden of pain. When you feel suicidal, you are accepting a very distorted view of yourself, and rejecting the chance to improve your life. One day you will feel better, even happy, if you give yourself time. You might even become a stronger, more sensitive person as a result of this misery. Give yourself another chance.

Eating disorders

Stress often makes people eat more or less than usual. Some use food for comfort, reaching for a packet of crisps or a bar of chocolate when they are feeling down. Others don't want to eat at all when they are upset.

▲ **If you feel suicidal, calling an organization such as the Samaritans is an important first step in getting help.**

Sabina, seventeen, began eating more before her GCSEs.

'I started having extra snacks while I was revising to take my mind off the boredom and tension of studying. Then my mum would cook me huge meals "to keep me going". After the exams it was difficult to cut down. I felt so miserable about all the weight I'd gained, I ate even more. It didn't get better until my friend encouraged me to join an aerobics club.'

Most of us use food as a crutch at times. Occasionally, however, stress can lead to more serious eating disorders such as anorexia, where dieting gets out of control, or bulimia, where sufferers are trapped in a cycle of bingeing and vomiting. Anorexia particularly affects teenage girls. No matter how much weight they lose, sufferers see themselves as overweight. Some actually starve themselves to death; many have to be treated in hospital. Bulimics usually maintain a fairly normal weight, but can suffer from exhaustion, bad breath and loss of periods. Frequent vomiting erodes their tooth enamel.

Eating disorders don't have a single cause, but sufferers are often stressed and anxious. Anorexics are sometimes worried about growing up – controlling their eating habits makes them feel they have more control over life in general. Bulimics, on the other hand, often feel very out of control. They binge and vomit under stress, then have feelings of self-loathing and disgust. Both conditions need urgent treatment.

Stress is a normal part of life but too much is unhealthy and unpleasant. You can't avoid it entirely, but being aware of what can cause stress and what in particular makes you tense will help you to cope with your feelings. You can then find ways of making problems or stressful situations easier to deal with.

Physical changes

Puberty is a time of emotional and physical upheaval. You have to cope with your rapidly changing body, and you might often feel unsure if what is happening to you is normal. It's not surprising that many people find puberty an extremely stressful time.

Going through puberty earlier or later than everyone else can be one cause of stress. Being taller, shorter, thinner or fatter than your friends is worrying and it's not something you can hide! It will all even out, though, as you or your friends catch up. Girls develop faster than boys, often filling out before reaching adult height and so looking chubby for a while. Boys often grow up before they grow out and look lean and skinny

▲ **People don't all go through puberty at the same time. Looking different from your friends can make you feel anxious and self-conscious.**

for a year or two. You might hate the way you look now, but, like the ugly duckling, many a glamorous adult went through puberty looking decidedly ungorgeous.

Acne

Three-quarters of teenagers get spots. Hormones affect the oil-producing glands in the skin, blocking the ducts that lead to the surface and causing spots. Having acne is stressful. Although it looks worse to you than to everyone else, a bad complexion can make you feel even more self-conscious about your appearance.

Doctors can offer a range of treatments. Keep your skin clean, but don't over-wash, and avoid squeezing the spots, as this can cause scarring. A good diet and exercise might help. Try not to worry – it won't go on for ever.

What happens to girls

For most girls puberty begins at the age of eleven or twelve and ends at around the age of sixteen. Hormones such as oestrogen are produced in increased amounts, causing the growth of breasts and of hair around the genitals and armpits. You might also notice a clear or white vaginal discharge a year or two before your periods start. This is normal and it shouldn't be a problem if you wash regularly and change your pants daily. However, check out any changes in colour or smell with your doctor, just to make sure you don't have an infection.

Teenage girls tend to store fat, especially on the breasts, thighs

Nick, fifteen, developed spots that spread over his face, back and chest.

'I tried creams, lotions, soaps, the lot, but nothing made much difference. I couldn't bear looking in the mirror and avoided going out if they were particularly bad. Eventually my doctor managed to help, but by that time my self-esteem had taken a real battering.'

and hips, giving more womanly curves. But in a society that worships thinness, girls often worry that this is excess weight. It isn't, and it will probably even out as you grow taller. Meanwhile, eat healthily and avoid crash diets, which create an obsession with food and often make you heavier in the long run. Try to love your new shape – others certainly will.

Periods

At puberty, your ovaries start releasing an egg into the womb roughly once a month. This is known as ovulation. If you have sex and the egg is fertilized by a male sperm, the egg implants itself in the womb lining. Every month, the lining of the womb thickens in preparation for this happening. If the egg isn't fertilized, the womb lining is shed

◀ **You might feel a mixture of anxiety and excitement when your periods start.**

close friend could advise you about using sanitary towels or tampons. Most schools also cover this as part of health education, so you should be able to start your periods knowing what is happening to you and how to manage.

Many girls worry about starting unexpectedly and staining their clothes. Signs that you are due include increased vaginal discharge, swollen breasts or stomach, and perhaps more spots. Some girls feel moody, tired or irritable just before a period, so make allowances for unsettled emotions. Change tampons or towels regularly to prevent leaking and smelling. Cramps, nausea and backache are common in the first few years. Exercise can help to relieve these problems, or you can try paracetamol or painkillers produced specially for painful periods. These are available from the chemist, but use them with care and never exceed the recommended amount. If none of these remedies help, see your doctor, who can try other treatments. There's no need to suffer in silence.

as menstrual blood, and the cycle begins again.

Most girls start their periods between the ages of ten and seventeen. Don't worry if your periods are irregular at first, even if there are gaps of two or three months. You should eventually settle into a cycle of a period lasting three to five days roughly every month. If your periods are usually regular, a missed or late period can be caused by stress, strenuous exercise, changes in diet, or even, of course, by pregnancy.

Your first period marks the start of womanhood and your ability to have a child. Your parents might worry about you getting pregnant or have mixed feelings about you growing up, and might feel too awkward or embarrassed to give you advice. An older sister or a

▲ Coping with periods at school can be stressful, especially if you are worried about other people making comments.

Once your cycle settles and becomes familiar, periods are less stressful. Many women see them as a positive celebration of their womanhood and fertility, and enjoy the rhythm they give to their lives.

Breasts

Girls often feel anxious about their breasts. It's normal, for instance, to have one bigger than the other, or for them to feel tender and lumpy before a period. Beautiful breasts come in all shapes and sizes, so try not to worry that your breasts are too large or too small.

Like fourteen-year-old Kate, you might feel self-conscious about having breasts at all.

'They suddenly appeared out of nowhere and seemed enormous! I thought everyone was staring at me all the time. I felt so self-conscious, I'd only wear baggy clothes. My mum came to the rescue though, helping me buy my first bras and boosting my confidence.'

What happens to boys

In boys, the hormone testosterone causes the scrotum to thicken and darken, and the testicles to develop. In childhood, the testicles are small and held close to the body; in adolescence they enlarge and 'drop' lower between the legs. Boys also develop more muscle, particularly around the shoulders, arms and chest, and grow hair on the genitals, armpits and face.

As the 'voice box', or larynx, grows, and your vocal cords lengthen and stretch, your voice will 'break' and deepen. This can happen quickly or take several years. The sudden tendency of the voice to swing from high to low can be embarrassing. In 70–80 per cent of boys, changing levels of hormones cause their chests to swell around the nipple. If this happens to you, don't panic. You are not changing sex and the swelling should disappear within eighteen months.

Erections and ejaculation

If periods mark the start of woman-hood, the ability to ejaculate signals the start of manhood. Most boys discover that they can ejaculate through masturbating or by having wet dreams.

Even babies get erections, but it's not until puberty that they become common. Stefan, for instance, was embarrassed by sudden, unwanted erections, often while sitting in class or watching television with his family. Eventually he confided in his dad, who advised him to concentrate on something else until the erection went away. Like Stefan, you will find erections become more manageable as your hormones settle down and you find sexual outlets such as masturbation or intercourse.

Wet dreams are common in adolescence – they are the body's way of releasing semen to make way for fresh sperm. Try sleeping on a towel, and don't worry too much about your parents finding out. You might want to die of embarrassment at the thought, but they are probably expecting it.

Boys often worry about the size of their penises. It's difficult to know what's 'normal', as penises look very different when unaroused. Nothing can change your penis size, but it makes no difference to your ability to have sex or to please a partner.

Everyone goes through puberty, but parents often forget how stressful it can be and treat it as a bit of a joke. After all, they know you'll soon grow out of it. Some parents find it difficult and embarrassing to discuss physical changes, but you need facts and, above all, reassurance. You can suggest they get you a book, or get information yourself from your library, doctor or school counsellor.

▶ **Worries about your changing body can cause more stress if you are unable to share your concerns.**

Sex

At puberty, it is not only your body that starts preparing for sexual relationships. You start to think more about finding a partner and exploring sex. It's an exciting time, but lack of information, or inaccurate information, can cause anxiety and stress.

There are lots of strange myths and attitudes concerning sex. Stick to facts, not what you hear in the playground. There is no proof that sex education encourages promiscuity, but plenty showing that good information reduces the number of unwanted pregnancies and people with sexually-transmitted diseases.

Some parents find it hard to accept that sexual behaviour at a relatively young age is fairly normal now. If you try to talk to them about sex, you might be met with shock, disapproval or embarrassment. Sometimes, parents are upset by the thought that they are no longer the most important people in your life, and they show these feelings as strictness or anxiety. They need time to adjust.

► **Different attitudes to sex can cause arguments between parents and teenagers.**

Masturbation

Masturbation, or 'wanking', is perfectly natural. It doesn't make you blind, stunt your growth, give you spots, or change your sexuality. It's considered fairly normal for boys, but most girls and women do it too.

Everyone fantasizes about sex. Where else will you have a passionate affair with a film star or a fling with that person in the sixth form? Fantasies are a safe place to work through your sexual feelings and explore what turns you on. Some people worry that their sexual fantasies are sick or perverse. Fantasies cannot harm you or anyone else – as long as they stay in the mind. Many people fantasize about things they wouldn't dream of doing in real life.

Contraception

For teenagers, sex often happens on the spur of the moment, and many adolescents think that pregnancy can't happen to them. It can. Unprotected sex can make a girl pregnant, no matter when, where or how you do it. Teenage girls are particularly fertile.

The only totally reliable contraceptive is not to have sex at all. If you do have sex, always take precautions. It might be embarrassing but that's nothing compared with the tragedy of an unwanted pregnancy.

If you do have unprotected intercourse, your doctor can prescribe the morning-after pill up to seventy-two hours afterwards.

Using contraception soon becomes second nature, leaving you free to relax and enjoy yourself. Show that you can take responsibility for your sexual feelings and actions by sorting out contraception before you have sex. Your doctor or local family planning clinic can give you information about the options, so you can pick the method that suits you. The doctor will not tell your parents or guardians, and there's no law that prevents young people from buying condoms.

Experimenting with sex
As long as you are careful to avoid HIV infection and pregnancy by using a condom,

▲ **If you do decide to have sex, always use a condom. You might feel embarrassed about buying and using them, but they can protect you against pregnancy and HIV infection.**

many people feel there is nothing wrong with exploring sex in adolescence. However, it's not something you should rush into. If in doubt, wait.

Your first time can be a real letdown, especially if you are not really ready for sex, or doing it because of pressure from your partner, because you are drunk, or just to see if you can. Don't expect too much, too soon. Good sex takes time, a partner you trust, privacy, freedom from anxiety and, above all, practice.

▼ No matter how much you love your partner, don't give in to pressure from him or her if you don't feel ready for a sexual relationship.

While boys worry about their performance, girls worry that sex will hurt. The hymen, the thin, elastic membrane covering the vagina, might break and cause slight pain and bleeding the first time you have intercourse. However, strenuous activity, such as playing sport, can cause the hymen to rupture long before you first have sex, so you might not notice this at all. Sex shouldn't hurt after the first few times – a vagina that can accommodate a baby's head can easily take an erect penis. If it is painful, you might both need to hold back until you are properly aroused. It might be that you are not really comfortable about having sex at all.

Getting pleasure from sex and reaching an orgasm can take girls some time. You need to be familiar with how your body works and what feels good, through foreplay or masturbation. You also need to feel entirely at ease and happy with what is happening, and to be with a sensitive partner you can talk to and who doesn't rush things.

Stress-free sex is planned and safe. Being responsible means wearing a condom and taking care of other people's feelings.

Don't pressurize someone into having sex, pretend you like someone to get him or her to sleep with you, or ignore him or her afterwards. Sex heightens emotions – bad experiences or rejection can scar for life. Remember to do as you would be done by.

Homosexuality

Most teenagers wonder occasionally if they are gay. Crushes on people of the same sex are common, and many adolescents experiment with homosexual sex before settling down into a 'straight' lifestyle. It's just another way of expressing affection and exploring sexual behaviour, and it doesn't mean you are gay.

However, you might realize that you are not just 'going through a phase', and that you do prefer people of the same sex, or that you have sexual feelings for both men and women. This can be very hard to accept, especially as many teenagers aren't very tolerant of homosexuality.

▲ **Don't worry if you feel unsure of your sexuality — many people experience this during adolescence.**

Astrid, seventeen, was devastated when she finally realized she preferred girls to boys.

'I felt like a leper, and thought everyone would reject me. I kept quiet and went out with boys and pretended everything was okay. It seemed easier to hide how I felt, but it didn't do me any good in the long run.

'When I finally accepted my feelings towards other women, I felt a lot better about myself. I didn't care so much about what people thought. I began to meet other lesbians and started to feel proud of my sexuality. It's part of me and who I am. I don't announce the fact that I am a lesbian to the whole world but I no longer feel I have to hide it.'

It's difficult enough admitting you are gay to yourself; it can be even harder to tell your family and friends. Attitudes are changing, but you might still meet rejection and prejudice just when you most need love and support. Parents can find it particularly difficult to accept. They might blame themselves for 'doing something wrong' when you were younger, or worry about your risk of getting Aids if you are a boy. They might be angry or hostile, or they might think it best to ignore what you have told them. They, too, have to face a different future – the longed-for wedding day or grandchildren might never happen.

Most people will come round to accepting your sexuality eventually, but it might take them some time.

Pregnancy

A missed period, swollen or tender breasts, nausea, vomiting and excessive tiredness are all early signs of pregnancy. You can buy a pregnancy test from the chemist that can give a result from the day your period is due. If you do test at this very early stage, though, you should repeat the test a few days later to be absolutely sure.

It is a bad idea to have a baby when you are a teenager. Physically, it's more risky for mother and baby than it is when you are older, but the main impact is on your life and emotions. Teenage mothers are less likely to stay on at school, or to have a stable relationship, and teenage fathers suffer too. Babies are hard work and put great strain on young relationships.

Laura discovered she was pregnant when she was fifteen. She had been seeing her boyfriend, Danny, for six months.

'It was the most stressful thing that had ever happened to me. One moment I wanted to keep the baby, the next I just wanted an abortion. My parents were furious at first, then very worried for me. I found it almost impossible to make a decision, but I miscarried at nine weeks anyway. I still wish I'd never let it happen at all.'

They don't instantly bring love or meaning into your life, and they considerably reduce the choices open to you. Nor is abortion an easy option. It can be emotionally devastating and is not without risk, especially later in pregnancy.

If you are pregnant, you need to make a decision reasonably fast. Take a deep breath and tell your parents. Talk it over with them and those close to you. You need to think carefully about the impact a baby will have on your plans for the future, and about the options that are open to you. If necessary, ask your doctor to refer you to a counsellor, who can help you get things clear in your mind.

Boys, unfortunately, have to accept that the decision rests with the girl. All a boy can do is make his wishes known.

Sexually-transmitted diseases

Everyone fears HIV, but there are plenty of other unpleasant diseases that can be picked up through sexual contact. Herpes, for example, is incurable, chlamydia can lead to infertility and genital warts are linked to cervical cancer. See a doctor if you experience pain on urinating, unusual discharge from the penis or vagina, or itching, lumps, blisters or sores around the genitals. Don't assume the symptoms will just clear up – even if they do, it doesn't mean the

disease has gone. Treatment is free and confidential. If you do have an infection, you must tell your partner.

HIV, which can lead to Aids, is not a homosexual disease. In some countries, it's more common among straight people than among gays. HIV is passed by contact with infected semen or blood. People might not have symptoms for up to ten years after they become infected.

▲ Telling your parents you are pregnant will be difficult but they might be able to help you decide what to do.

Anyone can catch HIV or other sexually-transmitted diseases. Prevention is definitely better than cure, so avoid casual sex and always use a condom. Some girls worry that boys will think less of them if they carry, or suggest using, a condom. It's probably not wise to sleep with someone immature enough to think like that anyway.

Rape and sexual abuse

Rape and sexual abuse are disturbingly common. The helpline Childline, for instance, gets over 10,000 calls a year from young people saying they have been sexually abused. Most victims are raped or abused by someone they know, often a member of the family or a close family friend.

Victims often say nothing. On top of the horror of their experience, they often feel frightened, guilty, and ashamed, fearing they won't be believed, that it would cause too much trouble if they told anyone, or even that it was somehow their fault. But without help, a traumatic experience like this can affect your sexuality and relationships for many years.

Sometimes people aren't sure if they have been abused. Ask yourself if it made you feel uncomfortable or hurt you. Did the other person ask or threaten you to keep it secret? Did he or she

ignore your requests to stop? It doesn't matter if you were going out with the person – he or she was wrong to carry on if you had asked him or her not to. It was not your fault.

If you are assaulted, go to the police or social services, or tell a relative, doctor or teacher. Alternatively, ring your local rape crisis centre or Childline. It's very important to talk to someone who understands how you are feeling, someone who can reassure you

that your feelings are normal. If the police are told, you will be asked to make a statement and might be examined by a doctor. If the police cannot collect enough evidence to bring charges, or the case fails in court, at least you will have put the abuser off doing it to you or anyone else again.

▼ **Victims of abuse often feel too frightened and ashamed to tell anyone what has happened to them.**

Relationships

Many adolescents are desperate to have a boyfriend or girlfriend, feeling that it will give them confidence in their own attractiveness and impress their friends. Going out with someone is also a signal to your family that you are growing up and no longer 'just a kid'.

It's good to explore and experiment while you are young, but rushing into relationships can leave you with little time and energy for school work, friends and other interests. It's also better to wait for someone worthwhile than to dent your confidence in a series of casual relationships.

Friends

For most teenagers, friends are as important as parents or partners. They are the people you hang out with, sharing your secrets and talking endlessly about everything under the sun. They are often the people you turn to when you are hurt, angry or disappointed. Life without friends can be very bleak.

It has been estimated that a fifth of young people find it hard to make friends. Everyone has times when they feel lonely, particularly in a new school or new area. It's stressful, but being lonely isn't a

▼ **Friends are very important, especially during your teenage years when you really need people who understand how you feel.**

life sentence – there is something you can do about it. Be prepared to make the first move, and give it time. No one likes to feel under pressure to form new friendships too soon. Try developing characteristics that people find attractive – confidence, cheerfulness and friendliness.

People who seem at ease with themselves and genuinely interested in other people usually find it easier to make friends. Often the most popular adults developed their attractive personalities or wonderful sense of humour because they felt left out when they were younger.

Attractiveness

Most teenagers worry about how they look, and convince themselves that they will never have a boyfriend or girlfriend because they are too unattractive. We are bombarded everywhere with images of perfect women and men, and it's impossible not to judge ourselves against those ideals. But no one really looks that good, not even the models themselves. Make-up, lighting and clever photography can make most people look stunning.

Beauty really is in the eyes of the beholder. Lots of things that have nothing to do with the way they look make people attractive, such as kindness, confidence, or a sense of humour. Having qualities like these will make you happier in the long run than a lovely face or a gorgeous figure. As you get older, you'll become more relaxed about your looks and appreciate that we are all different. You'll also find that we are all looking for something different in a partner. Very few people want to stay in a relationship just because they have a partner who looks wonderful.

Breaking up

Breaking up is always stressful. Being rejected, turned down or stood up is a painful blow to your self-esteem, however sensitively the other person handles it. Adults have the experience to know they'll recover from rejection, but young people are more vulnerable, especially when going out with someone is often seen as the key to popularity. Early relationships nearly always fail, and it's usually no one's fault. Your boyfriend or girlfriend perhaps didn't want the same level of affection or commitment as you, or one of you might have met someone else. Sometimes, relationships just reach their natural end. It's not a failure if you had a good time while it lasted.

Carol, fifteen, went out with Carl for six months before he told her he'd met someone else.

'I've never been so upset. I couldn't stop crying and didn't want to eat anything. It hurt so much and I felt so embarrassed. I skived off school for a week, because I couldn't face seeing my friends. My heart and stomach actually ached from the pain.

'Of course, I did start to feel better after a while, but splitting up really knocked my confidence. It was a long time before I felt ready to go out with anyone again.'

Teenage affairs seem very serious at the time because the experiences are new to you. It's a cliché to say you'll get older, wiser and tougher, but it's true. You will meet other people, and probably one day you will meet someone you can settle down with. In the meantime, find people you can talk to about your feelings. Treat yourself to something that boosts your confidence. Tell your family what has happened – you might be surprised at how supportive they are. Rushing straight into another relationship is inviting disaster. You might want to prove you don't need your ex, but you risk another rejection or hurting someone else's feelings.

Some parents seem hardhearted about teenage relationships, saying there are plenty more fish in the sea. It might not make you feel better, but they are right. They know that in a matter of months you won't give your ex a second thought. It's unlikely that your father was the first person your mother met, and vice versa. They've loved and lost and survived to tell the tale, and they know you will too.

▶ **Splitting up with a boyfriend or girlfriend is difficult, but it's better than staying in a relationship where you might get really hurt.**

Bad relationships

Ambrose was seventeen when he met Karen. At first things were fine, but she began criticizing him and putting him down in front of her friends. She would stand him up at the last minute or, when they did go out together, flirt with his friends.

'I really liked her, and tried to please her, buying her flowers and offering to take her to the cinema. But it seemed the harder I tried, the worse she got. Eventually my dad asked me what was going on, and I realized it had to end.'

Many of us find ourselves, like Ambrose (left), in a bad relationship at some point. Honesty in a relationship is a good thing, but that doesn't mean you have to put up with your boyfriend or girlfriend criticizing your every tiny fault. Partners should be supportive and boost your confidence. You deserve decent treatment, so if someone messes you about, or the relationship causes you more pain than pleasure, get out. The sooner you do, the sooner you'll meet someone worthwhile.

Unfortunately, abusive relationships are common. If you meet someone who starts hitting you or forcing you to do things against your will, leave him or her immediately, because this person has more problems than you can deal with. Your relationship might have been wonderful in the beginning, but it won't be in the future – no matter how much he or she begs, apologizes or promises, the abuse will get worse. If you haven't the strength to end the relationship, tell someone you can trust and ask for help.

It's tempting to believe you can help or change someone with a 'problem', such as thieving, joy-riding or drug addiction, but it's unlikely that you can. Ask him or her to stop. If he or she doesn't, leave before you get hurt.

Promiscuity

Sometimes, people sleep around in an attempt to reassure themselves that they are attractive or popular. It can be a way of expressing unhappiness or of trying to get power over others.

Sleeping around can be harmful to your health and to your emotions. With the right person, sex can feel close and loving, but being promiscuous can lower your self-esteem. Making love with someone who is not really interested in you can make you

▲ **Having sex with the wrong person can make you feel worthless and very unhappy.**

feel worthless and used. It's much better to learn about giving and receiving sexual pleasure in a loving environment.

That said, we all do things we later regret. If you find yourself wishing you hadn't slept with someone, think about why you did it. When you are more clear about your reasons, you can avoid making the same mistake again.

Families

Families can be the greatest source of stress in our lives. Unfortunately, adolescence, with its physical and emotional upheavals, often coincides with parents' approach to middle age. Mothers might be feeling physically unwell, if they are going through the menopause. Both parents might be worrying about their continuing attractiveness, or about their career prospects, or coping with ageing parents of their own. They might not be feeling very level-headed themselves.

It's a fact of life that teenagers and parents argue, and it's stressful for everyone involved. The areas of dispute can seem endless: school work, friends, girlfriends or boyfriends, clothes, diet, money, housework – most families cover all of these at some point. Some teenagers think their parents are too strict, others complain that their parents are too busy to care about them. Some parents have double standards, expecting sons to do less housework and giving them more freedom than daughters.

In finding your own identity, you might reject the habits and values of your parents. You start to see them as ordinary people who make mistakes like anyone else. You can begin to argue clearly for what you want and believe. While it's natural for you to question and challenge your parents' views, it can feel threatening to them. They might feel you are rejecting them.

Certain things probably wind you up: being treated like a kid, lack of privacy, parents who interfere. Anger and confusion can make

Parvin, fourteen, was constantly fighting with her mother.

'We argued all the time, over anything and everything. Whatever I wanted to do, she disapproved of. She didn't like the way I looked and she didn't care what I thought. She was always nagging me about things. I got so sick of it, I'd just stay in my room until meal times.

'When we did get into arguments, one of us would end up in tears. I felt really awful seeing Mum cry, but it also made me feel really trapped and angry too.'

you feel like behaving badly, but any bad feeling that you cause in the family will have an impact on you. Tell your parents how you feel, rather than criticizing them. Be clear about exactly what you want and why. For example, it's better to say you want to spend more time with your friends at weekends than just to declare you want more independence. If you do start to get angry, take a deep breath and count to ten before you say anything.

Remember that parents worry. They held you as a helpless bundle in their arms, and they don't necessarily have less to worry about as you grow up. They still see danger lurking around every corner. When a toddler makes a bolt for a busy road, a parent's first reactions are panic, then anger. It's the same if you come home late without phoning. Your parents' emotions go into overdrive as they imagine you lying beaten in a gutter or slumped in a crashed car. You know you can take care of yourself, but parents find it hard to let go. Earn their trust by showing them you can behave sensibly and responsibly.

Don't forget your parents have a valuable resource – experience. They've had a chance to learn from their blunders. They can see dangers and disappointment of which you might not be aware. It's natural for them to want to stop you making your own mistakes. All parents have hopes and dreams for their children, and it might take them time to accept that you have different ideas.

▲ **You might get on better with your parents if you try to explain your point of view, instead of getting angry.**

▼ A part-time job is a good way to earn some extra money.

Rules

All families have rules, like keeping the living area tidy or turning up promptly for meals. These rules are often unspoken and unique to each family. Some things, however, infuriate most parents: messy rooms, loud music, spending hours on the phone, rudeness, lack of consideration and warfare between brothers and sisters. It's easy to get into a vicious circle. Your parents feel they have the right to lay down the law about certain things and nag because they feel they are being ignored. You stop listening because you feel they are always giving you a hard time.

Try to treat your parents with the politeness, honesty and respect you expect from them. Gaining independence means accepting the responsibility that goes with it and being prepared to contribute. Your parents are people – not just cooks, cleaners and moneylenders. Don't leave the house in a constant mess and expect them to clear it up. Appreciate the trouble they take over a meal and offer to cook once in a while. Make sure you are in when you say you will be. If you think your parents are unfair or expect too much, discuss it with them. Ask them to explain their reasons and be prepared to explain yours. Be willing to compromise.

Money is always a difficult issue. You want enough to be able to go out with friends or to buy what you need, but few parents have unlimited funds. Make a list of everything you need money for and agree with your parents who should pay for what. If you really do need more than they can afford, then, if you are old enough, you can discuss getting a part-time job.

Brothers and sisters

Even if you got on well with your brothers and sisters when you were younger, these relationships come under a lot of strain during the teenage years. Constant fighting, teasing and bickering are stressful for you and your parents. Life will be a lot easier if you can sort out your differences with your brothers and sisters. That might mean accepting that you don't like each other, and agreeing to keep your distance. Try to be polite and patient. Hopefully your relationship will improve in time.

Family crises

Rows are normal, but crises such as bereavement, family break-up or divorce, and unemployment can make things a lot worse. A family break-up is particularly stressful. It can be better than living in an atmosphere of tension and hostility, but it usually involves a lot of upheaval and means seeing less of one parent. Financial difficulties often follow, adding to the heartache. It's common to feel angry, rejected or betrayed and to want to punish one or both parents for making things so bad.

Jamie was twelve when his father left home.

'It all seemed to happen so suddenly. My mother was devastated and often wanted to talk to me about how she felt. It was terrible seeing her so upset. I felt really sorry for her but I didn't know how to help. I felt angry with Dad for hurting her, but I also missed him and needed his support. I felt really torn and didn't know who to talk to about it.'

Some people feel responsible for an abandoned parent, who might be grieving, hurt or angry. Although you might be pleased that your parents turn to you in times of need, you should lean on them rather than the other way round. You might need to ask a relative or family friend to help find someone else for your parents to talk to.

▼ **A family break-up is very stressful, especially if you are not sure what is going to happen to you. Let your parents know how you feel.**

When it comes to deciding who you live with, make your feelings known. It's hard to choose, but you must look after your own best interests. One solution might be to split your time equally between both parents, but be aware of the strain this might put on you. Try not to take sides in arguments between your parents, and find someone you can talk to about your feelings.

Bereavement

The death of a close family member is obviously very difficult to cope with, and is a time of great stress for everyone. Losing a parent, for instance, means adjusting familiar habits and routines. You might have to take on a lot more responsibility around the house. Grief is very tiring, and you and your family will be distressed and probably short-tempered for some time. Try to be as patient as you can. Things will get better.

New partners

If one or both of your parents remarry, or one meets a new partner who comes to live with you, getting used to the new situation can be as stressful as coping with your parents' original break-up. It's especially hard if you had hoped your parents would get back together, or if you had enjoyed your role as man or woman of the house and now feel rejected.

Stepfamilies can cause all sorts of problems. You are faced with someone else taking a parent's place, and perhaps with stepbrothers and stepsisters too. When two families combine you are bound to go through a stormy period as you all adjust your habits and expectations. Some difficulties are inevitable as you try to find a way of living together.

If you do get on with your mum's or dad's new partner, you might feel you are betraying your other parent. It's hard too if you really dislike your step-parent, but try not to make him or her the scapegoat for your bad feelings. Give the relationship time to develop. He or she is probably as confused as you are, and desperate to make things work between you.

▲ **Some teenagers enjoy spending time with their step-parents.**

School

The change from primary to secondary school usually comes as you enter puberty, making life quite stressful for a while. Secondary school is quite different from primary school, with a more structured day, more homework, and the need to make plans for life after you leave school. You move from being one of the oldest at school to being one of the youngest once again, and, as secondary schools are usually bigger than primary schools, you find yourself surrounded by crowds of strangers. If there is a choice of schools in your area, you might find several close friends have moved to a different one.

Pressure

As you move up through school, the pressure to do well increases. Some teenagers respond positively, but others don't. It's hard if you find it difficult to keep up, but people who do well at school can suffer stress too. They might be left out socially, or come under a lot of pressure to keep up their performance. Not all teenagers who are intelligent succeed at school. If there are problems at home, for instance, it's harder to focus on school work and do well.

Parents can make life at school better or worse. Some parents expect you to succeed at school because they did well themselves, or because your brothers or sisters got good grades. Others want you to succeed in certain subjects. Although it's natural to want the

▲ **It's harder to concentrate and do well if you work for too long without a break.**

best for your children, it's not fair of parents to load on the pressure. Like Paulo, you might have to get someone to help you explain to them how you feel.

Paulo, fifteen, was under a lot of pressure from his dad to achieve good grades in his exams.

'It was really awful. He would insist on checking my homework and rang up the teacher if he didn't agree with what we were covering. It got really embarrassing. In the end I asked Mum to tell him how much it was bothering me. She thought it was because he didn't do very well at school himself.'

Homework can be a real source of stress. Having the television or music on might make it more bearable, but you might find you can do the work in half the time with more peace and quiet. Try getting homework done early. Ask for help if you get stuck, rather than guessing or falling behind.

Learning difficulties

School problems are common, and have little to do with intelligence. Some people, for instance, suffer from learning difficulties such as dyslexia or 'word blindness', or find it hard to concentrate. They are not stupid, but they have a problem that makes it harder for them to learn. Most teachers are now aware of conditions like these and can deal with them effectively. Although it's embarrassing to admit that you are having trouble keeping up, it's better than falling behind or feeling like a failure.

Truanting

Teenagers begin truanting for all sorts of reasons. Many adolescents say they can't see the point of going to school, because they feel that what they learn at school has little to do with real life. To some extent this is true. Few of us use trigonometry or the principles of coastal erosion in adulthood. It can be hard to see the point of it all. However, you are likely to need qualifications to do what you

Owen, fourteen, started skipping school occasionally when he was having an off-day or he just couldn't be bothered to go, but it quickly became a habit to bunk off and hang around the town centre with a couple of friends. Several of Owen's teachers tackled him about his truanting, but he took no notice until the school sent an education welfare officer to talk to him and his parents. The officer explained that she would help Owen through any problems.

want. The exams might seem irrelevant, but they show that you can apply yourself and learn. And school isn't just about absorbing facts. It teaches you how to fit into a complex organization, which will be helpful when you start a job and have to get used to your workplace. At school, you also develop social and working relationships with other people. It's a safe environment to practise the skills you'll need in adulthood, such as meeting deadlines and working in teams.

You might find school an awful place to be, especially if you are falling behind in your work, having problems with a teacher, or being bullied. But truanting will lead to more trouble. It's much better to try to resolve your problems with a teacher or your parents now.

Sometimes stress about school can increase until you feel too ill or frightened to go. You need help overcoming this. The further you fall behind in your work, and the more you lose touch with your friends, the harder it will be for you to go back.

Exams

Many teenagers see their doctor around exam time because of headaches and other stress-related symptoms. Exams are a strain for everyone. You can destroy five years' work in three hours, and they are particularly hard if you don't have a good memory.

Try to keep stress to a minimum with good study and revision habits – ask your teachers for advice if you aren't sure how to go about revising sensibly. Keep things in proportion – most exams can be retaken.

Bullying and teasing

Persistent bullying or teasing is very stressful. It can destroy your confidence, making you feel weak and helpless. You might think that it's somehow your fault or that there's something wrong with you. There isn't. It is always the bully who has the problem.

Dealing with bullying or teasing is not easy, but you have to act. The longer the situation goes on, the harder it will be to sort out. If you don't put a stop to it, you are protecting the bully. Tell a teacher or relative what is going on and ask him or her for help. You are not being wet or cowardly by involving an adult; reporting a bully is an act of maturity and courage, and you are also helping all the bully's other victims.

When Lucy's GCSEs were coming up, she found she became increasingly anxious and panicky.

'It was awful. I spent all my time revising, but it just got harder. I'd read the same page over and over again without knowing what it was about. I got so tired I could hardly think. When it came to the exams I was all right, but I think I'd have done better if I could have relaxed more.'

◄ **Most people find exams stressful but you will probably achieve better results if you can keep calm.**

Who am I?

Identity crises are more or less compulsory in adolescence. You are moving from a child's view of the world to an adult's view and facing a mass of new ideas and experiences. You are exploring sexuality and relationships, and you might be thinking about issues such as politics or your religious beliefs. There will inevitably be times when life seems very complicated, and you feel very lonely and unsure of yourself.

Exploring ideas

Exploring and experimenting are healthier than adopting your parents' attitudes and values without thought. Children tend to accept their parents' views, but as they grow up they form opinions and values of their own. Some parents find it difficult to have you question their beliefs, but you need to look at the options, to pick and choose what's right for you. That means making mistakes. Even if you are not sure of your own judgement, you don't want someone else making decisions for you.

Some young people are afraid of taking risks. They avoid challenging situations or blame other people for their failures. They fear the consequences of a mistake or a blow to their self-esteem. Parents often want to protect their children from pain, disappointment or failure and find it hard to let go. But people learn through trial and error. It's part of how we grow up.

Making choices

Adolescence is about making serious choices about your career, relationships and lifestyle. Choosing is often stressful – you can't be sure that you're getting it right. You might find you often can't decide what to do, making plans one minute and abandoning them the next.

◄ It is normal for teenagers to experiment with different lifestyles, attitudes and ideas as they are growing up. Parents often worry about this but for teenagers it's an important step in becoming independent.

Josie, eighteen, had always wanted to be a ballet dancer, and studied hard to pass the necessary exams. But as she got older she found that the training required too much commitment.

'When I was younger, everything seemed possible. I thought that if I wanted to become a dancer, I could. But as I got older, I realized how difficult it is to achieve something like that. I had to face the fact that we all have limitations, and not everyone can be what they dreamed of.'

As you get older, it's natural to worry about your ability to fulfil even modest ambitions. For some teenagers, on the other hand, there is the dilemma of not knowing what they want to do. Not all choices concern careers, of course. Growing up also means accepting that you can't do exactly as you please. Your actions have consequences for yourself and other people, and we all have to take responsibility for what we do.

Your parents

All teenagers think that adults don't understand them, and to some extent this is true. Adults soon forget what it is like to be young, when you are constantly

▲ **Some parents find it hard to understand ideas and behaviour that is very different from their own. You might just have to agree to differ.**

trying out new ideas and rejecting them. Parents, who have probably settled firmly into the habits and attitudes with which they feel comfortable, can find this bewildering. Some love a good argument and will challenge your views as readily as you do theirs; others are more set in their ways and see your disagreement as a threat. Sometimes you just have to accept that your parents have a different point of view.

The future

Leaving school is an important stage in your movement from childhood to adulthood, but the initial excitement can quickly wear off if you are not sure what to do next or if you are waiting for exam results. Your expectations might be high, but so might your anxieties. You now have some choices about what you make of your life.

Further education

College or university is not like school. You are treated much more as an adult. It's up to you, for instance, if you miss lectures or classes, but if you do this, you might risk losing your place. For many people, their first months at college are some of the loneliest and most stressful of their lives. You have to cope with your new independence and responsibility, and make new friends. Leaving behind everyone and everything you know can make you feel very homesick. Remember that everyone else is, or has been, in the same boat; most people soon feel better and find their feet.

Your parents know you've grown up while you've been away at college, so they might expect you to show more responsibility and consideration. You, however, might feel they should trust you and not expect you to say where you are going or when you'll get in. Talk to each other. It's no longer appropriate for your parents to treat you like a kid. Nor is it right for you to treat home like a hotel. You might all need to compromise.

Work

Getting a job is often difficult. There is a lot of competition for most jobs, so avoid the stress of constant rejection by finding out exactly what the job you want requires. Then you can decide if it's worth pursuing.

Sam, eighteen, found that going to college can cause friction with parents.

'I went to university some way from home, but came back for the holidays. I really missed my family, but coming home was awful at first. I felt independent, but my parents still kept on about me going out and not helping enough around the house. My dad said that so long as I was still relying on them for my grant and a bed during the holidays, they had the right to tell me what to do. It drove me mad.'

When Joe left school at eighteen he thought he could walk into any job he fancied, but soon found the reality very different.

'I was incredibly naïve. I thought enthusiasm would be enough, but it wasn't. There were hundreds like me to choose from. Most of the time I wouldn't even get an interview, and each time I was rejected my self-esteem sank lower.

'Eventually I went to see the local careers service and they gave me advice on how to improve my applications and prepare for interviews – things like trying to find out a bit about the company first, to show I was keen. I suppose it must have helped because I did get a job in the end.'

Unemployment

Work isn't called work for nothing. Even those who love their jobs can face Monday morning with reluctance. Sometimes the idea of being unemployed can seem quite appealing, but being jobless is a truly stressful, boring and depressing experience. It's not like being on holiday. You lack money and a sense of your place in the world. It's easy to become isolated from your friends. The unemployed suffer from frustration and lack of confidence, and are more likely to become ill.

Try not to fall into bad habits such as watching television or staying in bed until lunch time. You'll only feel worse. Accept offers of training or help looking for a job; it's better than doing nothing and might really improve your chances. Consider going back to college or trying to get into a completely different type of work.

In the meantime, develop your hobbies, try some voluntary work, or learn new skills such as word processing or a foreign language. Even if these aren't relevant to your chosen career, employers will be impressed that you have made the effort.

Gemma, nineteen, was out of work for two years while living at home.

'It was the worst time of my life. My parents were understanding and helped me out financially, but all the family worked so I was on my own all day. I felt useless and inadequate. The more I got rejected, the more hopeless I felt.

'Eventually my dad found me a temporary job in his office, and after six months they decided to keep me on. It's not the best job in the world, but anything's better than having nothing to do all day.'

▲ If you have had no luck in finding a job, it might be worth going back to college. Better qualifications and training could give you the chance you need.

Leaving home

Moving out is often the biggest milestone on the road to adulthood for you and your parents, and there's usually a mixture of sadness and relief on both sides.

Unfortunately, many people leave home without knowing how to cook, clean, shop or balance their budgets, and don't realize how much they took for granted at home. Some overdose on the freedom, staying up all night or eating chips with every meal, but soon find out why these things are not a good idea.

Financial independence can be difficult. You are unlikely to be well off, and there seems an endless list of things to pay for before even considering clothes, holidays or a social life. Budgeting isn't complicated, but it can cause a lot of stress if you don't do it sensibly. Write down how much you have coming in and what you need to pay for. You'll soon build up a picture of what you can and can't afford. If you get into real difficulties, your student union or a citizen's advice bureau might be able to give you some advice.

▼ **Using your time and money sensibly is probably the last thing you want to do when you first leave home, but life quickly becomes stressful if you can't pay your rent or bills.**

Dealing with stress

Managing stress effectively means knowing exactly what's causing it and what you can do about it. Sometimes you can remove the source of the stress altogether, but many of life's problems aren't so easily solved. You might have to settle for improving either the situation or the way you deal with it.

Self-help

Sometimes stress is caused by events you can do little about, such as bereavement or illness. In these cases, just talking it over can be the best remedy of all. Someone else can often see your problems more clearly; if you have difficult decisions to make, he or she can help you work out what you need to do.

Alison, seventeen, found she wasn't anxious about anything in particular, but little things would build up and get on top of her.

'I might have a row with my dad and it would be raining. Silly things could make me feel really miserable. Often I'd treat myself to a new top or a haircut to snap myself out of it. Pampering myself still makes me feel better.'

If you often feel anxious, writing down what is worrying you can help put your anxieties into perspective. Often people get stressed about things they fear, but which are unlikely to happen. Putting it on paper helps you define the problem, how likely it is to occur, and what you can do about it.

▲ **Just writing down your worries helps you to get them in proportion and work out a way of dealing with them.**

You might find other things that help you through difficult moods caused by stress, such as exercise, trying not to be alone too much, or keeping up a routine. Sometimes, it's helpful to focus on the present rather than on what's happened in the past or might happen in the future. You might find that doing something positive about particular issues, such as joining an environmental group, makes those kinds of worry seem less overwhelming.

Coping skills

When something goes wrong, do you find yourself saying destructive things about yourself, thinking you are stupid or unattractive, or imagining people are saying things about you behind your back? We are often our own worst enemies. We all say and do things we could kick ourselves for afterwards, but a positive outlook means accepting that you can't be perfect and that sometimes things will go wrong. There's no point in getting angry with yourself for making mistakes; learn from them. Developing optimism and a sense of humour can do a lot to combat stress.

Other skills can make life run more smoothly. Being organized and keeping lists will help you remember to do things on time. Being tidy will save time and energy hunting for or replacing things you've mislaid.

▲ Life becomes much more enjoyable once you stop criticizing yourself.

Feeling panicky in particular situations can cause physical reactions such as blushing, sweating, or trembling. Remember that other people are unlikely to notice, and that each time you face the situation it will get easier and you'll feel more confident. Many people benefit from learning assertiveness, so that they can look after their needs and communicate effectively in stressful situations.

Dealing with change

Life is full of change, and change is stressful, even if it's something positive like going on holiday. Sometimes you need help to cope with it successfully.

> Eleven-year-old Theo was very anxious about changing schools.
>
> 'It was awful at first. Everything was so new and different, I didn't even know where to go for classes. But the school got older pupils to show us around and explain how things were done. We also had meetings where teachers explained things and asked us how we were coping.'

If you are not offered help, find out as much as you can about the change you are expecting. Talk to people who have gone through it about what they found difficult and how they coped. You might find there is a lot you can do to make things easier. Don't be afraid to ask for help. It's better to admit you're stuck than flounder on until you reach crisis point.

Healthy living

It's common to react to stress by drinking, smoking or eating more junk food, but these can make you feel tired and more likely to pick up illnesses. A good diet and healthy lifestyle will help your body cope with stress much better in the long run.

Exercise is one of life's great stress-beaters. It takes your mind off your problems and helps your body get rid of the tensions that build up. You'll look better, feel stronger and less tired, and feel much more confident. Activities such as swimming, jogging, brisk walking and aerobics are ideal if you don't want to take part in competitive sports, but make sure you train with qualified instructors and use the correct equipment.

Relaxation

Relaxation techniques, such as visualization or meditation, are effective ways of combating stress. There might be groups teaching these kinds of technique in your area – look in your local paper or library for information, or your doctor might be able to tell you who to contact. There are also books and tapes that can teach you the basic techniques.

▼ **Taking part in activities can help you to relax.**

However, relaxation isn't just about doing exercises. It's often helpful to find simple things that will take your mind off your problems. These could be anything from a long bath to going for a cycle ride.

Getting help

Many people try alternative therapies such as homoeopathy, reflexology, aromatherapy and acupuncture for stress-related problems. The treatments themselves are often very relaxing, especially those involving massage. The phone book lists people offering this kind of treatment, but it is likely to be quite expensive.

If things are really getting you down, your doctor can prescribe mild sedatives, sleeping pills or antidepressants. Alternatively he or she can put you in touch with someone who is trained to help you cope with stress or depression. A course of counselling or psycho-therapy might get you over a bad phase and give you the skills you need to deal with stress in the future.

The biggest problem with stress is its tendency to sneak up on us. Most people don't realize they are under too much pressure until the situation reaches crisis point. Coping with stress is about being aware of the tensions in your life and dealing with them before they build up too much. As you get older and become more familiar with what you can and cannot cope with, you might find stress becomes less of a problem. You can begin to turn it into a positive force, motivating you to change and improve your life.

▲ **Once you find ways to control stress, you can use it to help you perform better and meet new challenges.**

Glossary

abortion A medical operation to bring a pregnancy to an end.

acupuncture A therapy that uses needles placed on the body to treat a variety of illnesses.

Aids Acquired Immune Deficiency Syndrome – a fatal disease which can follow infection by the Human Immunodeficiency Virus (HIV).

antidepressant A drug used to treat depression.

aromatherapy A therapy that uses perfumed oils and massage to treat illnesses.

assertiveness Being able to make your needs clear to people without becoming angry and aggressive.

bereavement Loss through death of someone you care about.

bisexual Sexually attracted to both men and women.

condom A contraceptive rubber sheath placed over the penis.

counselling A form of therapy involving talking your problems through with a person who has been specially trained to help you deal with them.

depression Deep sadness or unhappiness.

dyslexia A learning disorder that makes it very difficult to learn to read and spell.

HIV Human Immunodeficiency Virus – a disease usually passed on through sexual contact or infected blood. It can lead to Aids, an illness which destroys the body's ability to fight off disease and infection.

homoeopathy A therapy that uses tiny amounts of natural drugs to cure disease.

homosexual Sexually attracted to people of your own sex.

hormone A natural chemical released by the body.

identity crisis A feeling of deep confusion that occurs when you are uncertain about some aspect of your personality and how you fit into the world around you.

meditation A form of relaxation often involving deep thought.

menopause The stage of life when a woman's periods stop and she is no longer able to become pregnant. Changing hormone levels can cause physical and emotional problems.

miscarriage Premature birth of a baby before it has a chance of survival.

oestrogen A female hormone that plays an important role during puberty in girls.

orgasm The moment of highest pleasure in sex, which is accompanied by ejaculation of semen in boys.

promiscuity Having lots of sexual partners.

psychotherapy Treatment of depression or mental illness by talking about the sufferer's thoughts and feelings.

puberty The stage of life when a child's body becomes sexually mature.

reflexology A therapy that treats the body through the feet.

sedative A drug that makes you feel calm.

suicide Causing your own death.

testosterone A male hormone that plays an important role during puberty in boys.

truanting Taking time off school without permission.

visualization A form of relaxation that involves imagining peaceful or positive scenes.

Further reading

Adolescence: The Survival Guide for Parents and Teenagers by Elizabeth Fenwick and Dr Tony Smith (Dorling Kindersley, 1993)

Bloody Kids! Bloody Parents! by Alex Justa and Glenn Rice (N & P Publishing, 1993)

Growing Pains by Dr David Bennett (Thorsons, 1987)

Growing Pains and How to Avoid Them – A Self-Help Book for Young People by Claire Rayner (Heinemann Quixote, 1984)

Surviving Adolescence: A Handbook for Adolescents and their Parents by Peter Bruggan and Charles O'Brian (Faber & Faber, 1986)

Thirteen Something: A Survivor's Guide by Jane Goldman (Piccadilly Press, 1988)

Where to get help

Anti-Bullying Campaign
10 Borough High Street
London SE1 9QQ
Helpline: 0171 378 1446
9.30-5 pm Mon-Fri
(Advice and counselling on bullying and how to cope)

Brook Advisory Centres
165 Gray's Inn Road
London WC1X 8UD
Tel: 0171 713 9000
(Can refer callers to 26 local centres providing contraceptive and counselling services for under-25s; 24-hour computerized helpline also available 0171 617 8000)

Childline
Freepost 1111
London N1 0BR Tel: 0800 1111
(24-hour free helpline for young people in trouble or danger)

Lesbian and Gay Switchboard
BM Switchboard
London WC1N 3XX
Tel: 0171 837 7324
(24-hour helpline providing confidential advice, information and counselling)

National Council for Voluntary Youth Services
Coborn House
3 Coborn Rd
London E3 2DA
Tel: 0181 980 5712
(Can help find a youth organization appropriate to caller's problem or query anywhere in England)

Rape Crisis Centres
Tel: 0171 837 1600
(Counselling or referral to local support groups)

Samaritans
Head Office
10 The Grove
Slough
Berks SL1 1QP
Tel: 0345 909090 or check phone book for local helpline.
(Confidential support to suicidal and despairing people)

Youth Aid
17 Brownhill Road
London SE6 2HG
Tel: 0181 697 2152/7435
(Advice, information and counselling for young people. Can refer to other agencies.)

Index